JOY IN SERVICE ON RUE TAGORE

PAUL MULDOON

JOY IN SERVICE ON RUE TAGORE

faber

First published in the UK in 2024
by Faber & Faber Ltd
The Bindery, 51 Hatton Garden
London EC1N 8HN
This paperback edition first published in 2024

First published in the USA in 2024
by Farrar, Straus and Giroux
120 Broadway, New York 10271

Typeset by Hamish Ironside
Printed in the UK by TJ Books Ltd, Padstow, Cornwall

A CIP record for this book is available from the British Library

ISBN 978–0–571–38602–4

Printed and bound in the UK on FSC® certified paper in line with our continuing
commitment to ethical business practices, sustainability and the environment.
For further information see faber.co.uk/environmental-policy

10 9 8 7 6 5 4 3 2 1

We do not ride on the railroad; it rides upon us. Did you ever think what those sleepers are that underlie the railroad? Each one is a man, an Irishman, or a Yankee man. The rails are laid on them, and they are covered with sand, and the cars run smoothly over them. They are sound sleepers, I assure you. And every few years a new lot is laid down and run over; so that, if some have the pleasure of riding on a rail, others have the misfortune to be ridden upon.

HENRY DAVID THOREAU, *Walden*

He who fights with monsters should look to it that he himself does not become a monster. And when you gaze long into an abyss, the abyss also gazes into you.

FRIEDRICH NIETZSCHE, *Beyond Good and Evil*

Contents

JOY IN SERVICE ON RUE TAGORE

The Spurs

It all began in a blur
of chalk and brine
that were hanging by a thread
over the ocean bed.
That's how I grew a spine.
That's how I won my spurs.
That's how I grew a spine.
That's how I won my spurs.

Since everything must stir
from a single cell
I kept trying to raise my head
from the ocean bed.
That's how I grew a shell.
That's how I won my spurs.
That's how I grew a shell.
That's how I won my spurs.

Long before my leather and fur
and wool were shorn
I was lying with legs spread
on the ocean bed.
That's how I grew a horn.
That's how I won my spurs.
That's how I grew a horn.
That's how I won my spurs.

Near Izium

for Andrey Kurkov

1

Our bunker was deep, set far back in the Soviet era,
yet a rocket attack on the airport at Dnipro
came through loud and clear. Despite our video link
being decidedly on the blink
we knew the plain of Donbas was a sheet of glass
over which all hell would shortly break loose.
Since Putin has but one item on his agenda
there is but one on our agenda—
to see him strung up for his crimes
against Ukraine as the perpetrators of the pogrom
at Babi Yar were to be strung up by their heels.
We must believe the wheel
will come full circle now we try to regroup
near Izium, even if reconstituting the wizened grapes
after which the city is named means we boil
more snow for water. Our faces glow with gun oil
and blood. Our very artillery might recoil
from the task at hand had we not been offered a rare
opportunity to teach Putin the error
of his ways and refute
his *Weltanschauung* that is, if anything, pre-Soviet.
Refute his worldview. If anything, pre-Soviet.

For this is one time we all must heed the call to arms
and stand absolutely firm
against the threat to what is no less my homeland
than yours. If I stood firm on Snake Island
or against the convoy Putin first sent to Izium
it's partly because my own Y chromosome
waves from the Pontic Steppe. A body finds a seam
at which to burst. Whosoever will order
such a mass murder
will not only be strung up by his heels but his nose
cut off for good measure. I'll spare you the minutiae.
The heels. The nose. I'll spare you the minutiae.
Let's just say that when a tank is bogged
down it takes a mere pocket
of resistance to consign that tank to the mire.
It turns out that if we must boil more
snow from the ditch
it'll be to the accompaniment of Shostakovich.
Live by white phosphorus, die by white phosphorus.
An oligarch nudging through the Bosphorus
would do well to consider returning to the commune.
His penis-yacht is registered in Grand Cayman.

September 1941. A fortnight after they threw a ring
of steel around Leningrad, the Nazis would fling
34,000 Jews into that ravine at Babi
Yar and cut them down. Toodle-pip.
No thought of offering a Jew a boobytrapped
chocolate bar with which they'd later reckon
on taking out Churchill. If all hell has again broken
loose over Babi Yar
it's because that particular jar
of honey has kept fresh. Babi Yar. That particular jar
has kept fresh for almost a century.
In addition to bombing schools and health centers,
Russia's desecrated the ravine Eberhard and Rasch
and Blobel first desecrated in 1941. Not Russia.
Putin. This is Putin's war. That moan is the moan
of a slave taken by the Ottomans
from the Lawless Fields. A time warp
in which Putin will scrub
the data on Gorbachev and perestroika.
When it comes to an air strike
on a school, not even his Ministry of Culture
has the nerve to suggest the damage is collateral.

4

To gaze out over the burning lake of Acheron
is to gaze at the ruins
of Liman and try to comprehend
how Putin has managed to overextend
himself so disastrously. He must believe the lance
is still used in battle given how his supply lines
have been disrupted. *Ní bhíonn smeara gan dealg*
is a notion any ideologue
should commit to memory before thinking to deploy
a forty-mile convoy
of vintage tanks. It may well be that Bellerophon
rode Pegasus over the heads of orphans
and widows. To cut down 34,000 Jews in the ravine
of Babi Yar is one thing but to wreck
the memorial's quite another. That's why an oligarch
nudging through the Bosphorus will be hunted down
and ridden out of town.
Nudge-nudge. Hunted down. Ridden out of town
on his own mast. It's not only over Donbas all hell
will break loose. Whosoever throws a body in a hole
and leaves one hand
sticking out must high-five it on the witness stand.

5

The idea that you can't have "blackberries
without the bramble-barbs" is one we must impress
upon any despot entering the lists
with his outmoded lance. The constant missile-blasts
over Mariupol and Mykolaiv
were meant to grind us down but we now believe
we can give even an asteroid
a corrective push. Air raid after air raid
may be meant to grind us down but NATO
has afforded us the wherewithal to coordinate
our artillery units.
A soundtrack of Shostakovich's quacks, hoots,
pants, and gasps. We will score a direct hit
on whosoever would desecrate
that memorial on the outskirts
of Kyiv. A sacred memorial. Always on the outskirts.
Though we've lived for months in a dank
basement while our antitank
guns have staved off Putin's bombardment,
living in that basement
and sleeping under the filthiest of bedspreads
will never dampen our spirits.

6

It may be that the Strategic Arms Limitation Talks
have reduced the risk that his own tinderbox
will blow up in Putin's face
yet he continues to threaten to light the fuse
as he tries to recreate the court of Peter the Great
in Leningrad, a Leningrad
complete with troubadours. We launch kamikaze
drones against Pegasus as one Ivan flung a goose
insult at a second Ivan
in that story by Nikolai Gogol. There'll be no haven
for those who've left a foot in a felt boot
sticking out of a pit.
Putin is destined to have one close call
after another as he strums his banjo-ukulele.
Let's not forget it was Gogol
who invented the term *poshlost* for the all-time-low
that's now our permanent state. Yet we'll deal a blow
that will leave our would-be Tsar
in further disarray.
Our would-be Tsar. *Poshlost*. Total disarray.
He'll find it hard to simultaneously strum and pick
with his hands tied behind his back.

7

Now Putin has had to abandon so much matériel
as he's been ridden out of town on a rail
he's taken notice. Putin. His name means both
"path" and "psychopath."
Widows and orphans are gathering fuel
in a blasted vale
while Bellerophon's given Pegasus free rein
to ride roughshod over Ukraine.
The grain loaded into a six-oar gig is the grain
the world's bakers
mix with sawdust for bread. When he plays poker
with a nuclear plant, Putin forgets it's Moscow
he'll lay waste. His poker-face and his death-mask
will be one and the same. Death-mask.
Poker-face. One and the same for Vladimir Putin.
So many drones have been flown courtesy of Biden
against his Black Sea fleet
it goes without saying all those who've followed Vlad
to the Lawless Fields must end up in clabber
to the knee. He's so low on missiles he uses Kalibrs
for any routine barrage.
He's still smarting from having lost that Crimea bridge.

8

To live on an installment plan in a pine wood
near Izium is to have a crash course in what's what.
White phosphorus. Phosphorus. White.
It's never too late to impress upon
a demagogue stockpiling chemical weapons
the wind can quickly take a nasty turn.
A combination of our jerry-rigged drones—
by which I may mean our *jury*-rigged drones—
and much superior artillery fire
will carry the day. The booby trap and the trip wire
may slightly impede us yet we're emboldened
to search out Piltdown's
willing executioners, the new Rasches, Eberhards,
and Blobels whom we'll bury in a backyard
with our fallen countrymen. I myself will call it quits
when their faces, too, are eaten off by cats
and dogs. Whosoever
has ordained that Ukraine suffer
strangulation must himself be put in a choke hold.
For it's time to call a complete halt
to Putin's escapades, time for him to count the cost
of his ill-thought-out plan for global conquest.

9

That we're now able to deliver a Molotov cocktail
by drone is an indicator of the scale
of our improvisation. We've learned to outmaneuver
Putin whilst living on the Never-Never.
That moan must be the moan
of one who's fallen foul of an antipersonnel mine
somehow left on the slip
where an oligarch's sloop
has put in. The supply line for Château Latour,
truffles, and caviar must be an artery
disrupted in the sense it'll be unclogged.
As for Putin himself, may he fetch up in a gulag
wearing a triangular armband
that stands for "knackered." I won't belabor the point
but he mustn't simply be put out to grass.
He must eat rat-rations. He must eat candle-grease.
Let his pillow be stuffed with gorse
and common broom.
Let him find no rest in the bosom of Abraham
but forever go off at half cock
across the Dnieper in a six- or eight-oared black gig.
Across the Dnieper. At half cock. A black gig.

Anonymous: A Blackbird

9th century

That this one smallish bird might fill
an amphitheater with the trill
of notes from its yellow bill
is truly awesome—

a shock
wave over Belfast Lough
from a branch already chockablock
with whin blossom.

The Belfast Pogrom: Some Observations

The shipyard workers are no lighter on their feet
than the linen workers who flock
to Ross's Mill on Odessa Street

to wrangle a bedsheet
out of sullen flax.
The shipyard workers are no lighter on their feet

than this newly launched ship of the fleet
laying about it with its fluke.
The linen workers on Odessa Street

look to his nosebag for the mummy wheat
that may raise a horse-king from his cart-catafalque.
The shipyard workers are no lighter on their feet

than when they greet
the Catholics among them with a wrist-flick
of nuts and bolts. In Ross's Mill on Odessa Street

the tradition of drinking whiskey neat
extends to the recent influx
of shipyard workers never lighter on their feet

than when they're driven back by the heat
from a house they've torched. The black snowflakes
that settle on the linen workers of Odessa Street

summon quite bittersweet
memories of a Catholic boy recently flogged
by the shipyard workers no lighter on their feet

than the parakeet
on his shoulder. The boy's back striped like the flag
flying over Ross's Mill on Odessa Street.

When it comes to beating a retreat
through a mass of blood and brain-flecks
the shipyard workers are no lighter on their feet
than the linen workers of Odessa Street.

The Hula Hoop

1

The last wolf in Ulster was killed
in 1793, the year of the passing of the Relief Act
whereby a Catholic priest and his acolyte
could now conduct

Mass, if only in a building without a steeple
or maybe without a roof . . .
As of 1970 at least one constable
in the B-Specials had been heard to riff

on the idea of wheels within wheels
at Stormont. To be consigned to being "it"
in an eternal game of tig

was bad enough, far worse being that "free will"
was a concept now firmly ruled out
by a prophet taking the form of a three-legged dog.

2

A prophet taking the form of a three-legged dog
should have been a slam dunk
back in 1591 when the satirical poet Tadhg
Dall Ó hUiginn had his tongue

excised by the O'Haras for bad-mouthing their clan.
The introduction of the bus token
in Belfast in 1970 opened the route to Carr's Glen,
a territory but rarely retaken

since 1793, when meeting a footpad in the Fews
was still a dead cert.
This was one hundred years after Diego de Vargas

fought his way back into Santa Fe
in a supposedly "bloodless conquest" of the sort
I was now fated to forgo.

3

Once I was fated only to forgo
the mysteries of the Masons and the wheatear's
long rite of passage from sub-Saharan Africa
to Aghinlig. As the waters

broke over 1959
I was assured by the oracle
that none of my fellow Ulidians—none—
would be allowed to wriggle

out of trouble unless they were parttime
policemen. To be consigned to a birth canal
and remain eternally coiled

was bad enough, far worse being never to board
the 57 bus for Ligoniel
where that last wolf in Ulster was killed.

The River Is a Wave

The river is a wave that never breaks
though it may briefly surge
as it edges its way out of that three-mile-long lake
in which it's managed to submerge

its ever so slightly diminished sense of hurt.
The river is a wave that never breaks
despite such fitful spurts
of "enthusiasm." Let's say, for argument's sake,

that if it follows in its own wake
to satisfy an imperfectly remembered urge,
the river is a wave that never breaks
but is forever on the verge

of confronting an issue it's inclined to skirt
since it's only the sea, with its incomparable ache,
that may categorically assert
the river is a wave that never breaks.

Ducking for Apples

1

Working on the principle that possession
is nine-tenths of the law
I kneel facedown over a yellow basin

and set my sights on the choicest of a flotilla
of Laxton's Superbs. Were I to cramp
it in my teeth and duly

put it under my pillow I'd dream
tonight of the individual
who's my true love. The fact I've already one arm

tied behind my back dovetails
nicely with Solomon's idea that hope
deferred makes the heart sick. A glimpse of daffodils

through the birth-hoop.
What gazed back at Nietzsche was in fact Abyssinia
now he'd gazed so long into the abyss.

2

A glimpse of daffodils through the birth-hoop
reminds us of the meadows
in which Milo of Croton had us on the hip

long before we ever threw down wrestling mats.
That *malum* may refer to both "evil"
and "apple" muddies

the relationship between the apple blossom weevil
and the blossom stirring in the dark.
Even if a muezzin is mostly calling the faithful

to prayer he's keeping us all on track.
He, too, knows the apple is touted as an aphrodisiac
from as far as Tandragee

to a Tunis souk,
thereby flying in the face of the idea it's only hope
deferred makes the heart sick.

3

For if Nietzsche had gazed so long into the abyss
the abyss gazed back into him
it must reflect the place we gained sufficient poise

to get up on our gimpy
hind legs and swap a shady watering hole
for this new home from home

in the parish of Loughgall.
Our apple pie derives partly from Alsace-Lorraine
and partly from where it was left to cool

on a windowsill while Foghorn Leghorn
did the business
with a chicken hawk. The main lesson we'd learned

back there in Abyssinia
is that one out of five of these toothsome apple pies
is more likely than not poisoned.

When the Italians

Can we not, indeed, divide "grown-ups" into two distinct categories;
those in whom the child is most evident, and those resembling the boy?
WALTER DE LA MARE, "Rupert Brooke and the
Intellectual Imagination"

1

When the Italians invaded Libyan soil
they pioneered the dropping of bombs from a plane.
Shortly after the breakup of Standard Oil

Rockefeller himself had recoiled
from the notion it might have been preordained.
When the Italians invaded Libyan soil

they were at once metaphorically lancing a boil
and metaphorically opening a vein.
Shortly after the breakup of Standard Oil

the world would have been in considerable turmoil
even if the Italians had been able to refrain
from invading Libyan soil.

2

That same year Wharton published *Ethan Frome*,
her follow-up to *The House of Mirth*,
we'd see another push from Rome

to enlarge the dome
of the Pantheon till it encompassed the earth.
That same year Wharton published *Ethan Frome*

EP still composed in the sequence of a metronome.
Before Pound began to extend his turf
we'd see another push from Rome

and a going over of Treaties with a fine-tooth comb,
a dedication to *risorgimento* or "rebirth"
that same year Wharton published *Ethan Frome*.

3

Italian cinema will be playing catch-as-catch-can
to make sense of the bodies piled
in a partly constructed gas station in Milan

despite Visconti and Rossellini being in the van
because neither's lost the wide-eyed view of a child.
Italian cinema will be playing catch-as-catch-can

though a crowd of Communist partisans
is already pretty riled
in that partly constructed gas station in Milan.

Till it appeals to Cavalcanti, that perennial also-ran,
and his *dolce stil novo*, as it was itself styled,
Italian cinema will be playing catch-as-catch-can.

4

By 1945, the crowd will press in for a better look
through a Pirelli tire
at Mussolini's body hanging upside down by a hook

as if they might be inclined to cook
him over a slow fire.
The crowd will press in for a better look

at one who, until now, would brook
no argument. They agree the situation's pretty dire
for a body hanging upside down by a hook

like a goat hanging in a souk
in Tripoli. Now it's to admonish rather than admire
the crowd will press in for a better look.

5

In 1911, the Italians relied on newfangled aerofoils
to help broaden their definition of *Tramontane*.
Shortly after the breakup of Standard Oil

"To the victor belong the spoils!"
had become the rallying cry of every campaign.
When the Italians invaded Libyan soil

the cathedral in Milan saw at least one gargoyle
forced to cede such ground as it had gained
shortly after the breakup of Standard Oil;

the idea they might be embroiled
in a Hundred Years' War wasn't one they'd entertain
when the Italians invaded Libyan soil
shortly after the breakup of Standard Oil.

6

The bomber taking off from a coastal aerodrome
had tightened his girth.
We'd see another push from Rome

to distinguish *la schiuma*, meaning "foam,"
from *la spuma*, meaning "surf."
That same year Wharton published *Ethan Frome*

a skeleton in a catacomb
would jostle for an upper berth.
Though we'd see another push from Rome

only gradually did it hit home
Rockefeller had tripled or quadrupled his net worth.
That same year Wharton published *Ethan Frome*
we'd see another push from Rome.

7

It was surely not part of the grand plan
that Mussolini should dangle, disfigured and defiled,
in a partly constructed gas station in Milan,

his brainpan
crushed with a mallet but his expression not unmild.
Italian cinema will be playing catch-as-catch-can

till it finds some such melding of Li Po and Occitan
as made EP's poems haunting. Haunting and wild.
In a partly constructed gas station in Milan

love and death face off across a girder span;
till they're reconciled
Italian cinema will be playing catch-as-catch-can
in a partly constructed gas station in Milan.

8

In what is often disparagingly known as "a fluke
of history," it transpires
Mussolini's body's hanging upside down by a hook

in a gas station owned by Standard Oil. That kook
EP's been caged for preaching to the choir—
some of the very crowd pressing in for a look

at the outcome of the adventure they all undertook.
Only when his ankles are tied with piano wire
and his body's hanging upside down by a hook

will Mussolini's boyishness be brought to book:
any semirespectable neorealist director would hire
this crowd pressing in for a look
at Mussolini's body hanging upside down by a hook.

Horse Carpaccio

One remainder bin
at McNally Jackson was still full of straw
from the time Bess had wrangled a commercial tie-in

with the Grain and Feed Association. If there's a flaw
in the argument for heavy hors d'oeuvres
it's surely horse meat raw

as the sciatic nerve
that runs from Parma to Palermo.
"Lucretius knew a great poem embodies a swerve,"

Bess had ventured, "as a chariot horse must reaffirm
its first refusal on the field
against the Parthians." The squirm

of a peeled
shrimp offered by a Lufthansa *Flugbegleiter*.
American Grain and Feed no longer gave good yield

and were skittish about being underwriters
of this beano for Bess's *New and Selected Poems*.
She was now visibly slighter

than when she'd slow-danced a jeroboam
of Moët & Chandon
through the bookstore. Slow-danced a jeroboam

while singing Jacques Brel's "*Quand on
n'a que l'amour.*"
Partly because she was used to being abandoned

she favored a mare that was an easy doer
and could be turned out without being coddled.
"A whole other league from Brassens and Aznavour

though they all modeled
themselves on your fellow *Flugbegleiter*, J. S. Bach."
Even as American Grain and Feed dawdled

another woodcock
broke cover. "Brel? Must be a Belgian name.
I do know a 'gambrel' refers to both a horse's hock

and a hook for hanging game."
That had been at the *Horse Carpaccio* launch.
Partly because she herself was playing a long game

Bess had indeed become a byword for staunch.
Any page she'd written since was not just sliced thin
but sliced thin from her own haunch.

For Language and Brief Nudity

P A R S E P A R S E P A R S E P A R S E P
A R S E P A R S E P A R S E P A R S E P A
R S E P A R S E   A R S E   P A R S E P A R
S E P A R S E P A R S E P A R S E P A R S
E P A R S E P A R S E P A R S E P A R S E

Artichokes and Truffles

I have taken one more crack at the censors on the "oysters and snails" scene in Spartacus. Unfortunately, their objection to this scene is based upon the one remaining strong hold of their department which is an absolute taboo against portrayal of homosexuality . . . It is possible (although they will not say for certain) that they would pass the scene if we substituted "artichokes" and "truffles" for "oysters" and "snails."

EDDIE LEWIS to Kirk Douglas, February 25, 1959

1

What with the shitty crupper (a.k.a. the curple),
holding his saddle in place, the Emperor won't bristle
at the thought his Tyrian purple
derives from a snail rather than the glorified thistle
that is an artichoke. Would a mistle
have brought the thrush to dwell among us
or a thrush the mistle? Now the summary dismissal
of his thought that an hallucinogenic fungus
might throw up not only the Tungus
but the Tungusic shaman
has raised his hackles. Meanwhile a humongous
black truffle served by a priest or flamen
seems to have a male pig jostle
in the oak grove with a thrush (a.k.a. throstle).

2

A thrush sows the seeds, according to Erasmus,
that are the seeds of his own destruction;
this example of chiasmus
refers to the bird lime fluxion
on the very twig from which he causes the ruction
heard far beyond a grove of oaks.
The mistletoe attaches itself by means of suction
but its seeming rootlessness is enough to stoke
the rumor it has somehow thrown off the world-yoke.
The eight-legged horse on which he rode in
is enough to provoke
a reaction in Odin
that brings back Frigg and their ongoing friction.
The boiling of holly bark is illegal in this jurisdiction.

3

This oak grove is already the scene of a squabble
between the abbot of Cirencester,
who insists the globe artichoke was a bauble
brought to England in 1578 by some court jester,
and a druid now sequestered
in the ruins of the monastery who scans
the trees for corroborating evidence a quaestor
in Roman Britain had once fried artichokes in a pan
with a little nepitella. Even die-hard fans
admit the artichoke is but a pale shadow
of either the pinecone or the acorn glans;
two purple varieties (Imperial Star and Colorado)
may have been brought on in their cloister
by the first monks valiant enough to eat an oyster.

4

More likely, though, it was a Moorish farrier
rather than a monk
of any stripe who dared to cross the species barrier.
The Elder Pliny considered it a slam dunk
the artichoke was a monstrosity yet tried to debunk
the theory it was covered in mail
for that reason. An elephant with a tail in its trunk
will march in single file across the trail
of the air-breathing Cretan land snail
(a.k.a. *mastus*)
while wearing a breastplate of interlocking scales.
Stones give birth to stones, thought Theophrastus,
while Cicero put it about a truffle sprang
from where the earth had felt its own birth pang.

5

When Marcus Tullius Cicero was reincarnated
as Marc Bolan, it was as if a Jeep
had indeed dated
a Jaguar. That was a time when my old friend Beep
was Bolan's publicist and therefore able to reap
the benefits of the rock 'n' roll lifestyle.
The learning curve is spectacularly steep
when you're living in a stately pile.
It was, after all, Cicero who categorized the style
of Caesar's *Gallic*
Wars as "nude." The term "file"
derives from *filum* and may well refer to the metallic
thread beloved of so many of those chaps
who might well be into them ol' assless chaps.

6

Deepwater oysters are small, according to Pliny,
because it is dark and, in their dejection,
they look less for food. Such was my ignominy
when I realized I shared Tony Visconti's predilection
for adding a string section
to anything that stood still long enough,
I would myself move on. Having felt a tiny flexion
in his loins when he first saw Cynara in the buff,
Zeus had grabbed her by the scruff
of the neck and hauled her to his heavenly mansion.
Here's to a guy who sweats the small stuff
and queers the pitch of scansion
with a trochaic inversion, then takes a notion
to draw from a sea-snail the quintessence of ocean.

7

Pressed from the hypobranchial gland of the murex,
that dye propelled the ballista and battering ram
no less than the invention, after the war, of Lurex
had ushered in the age of glam.
Even as the artichoke was seen to cram
itself into the gully
of a most sacred grove so "Telegram Sam"
was flown in on a pulley
lest the Emperor lose face or be seen to sully
his reputation. His heart rendered for a nostrum,
the head and severed hands of Tully
were nailed to a rostrum
as a signal to those who might be inclined to ramp
up the volume on their Vampower amp.

8

Some version of Lurex was worn by Bolan
for even the stripped-down take on "Cosmic Dancer"
he sang at Wembley in 1972. If a semicolon
is the answer
to most punctuation woes, so a thrush is a prancer
on most mistletoe (a.k.a. "shit-twig")
that is sacred to that A-list necromancer,
the goddess Freya (a.k.a. Frigg).
Just as mistletoe spreads bird lime on a holly sprig
so Tully should have tempered his rhetoric
against Mr. Big.
We should also remember the fate of Vercingetorix
even as our idle chat around the soda dispenser
has come under the scrutiny of the censor.

9

It was Tantalus, in the first Olympian Ode of Pindar,
who allowed mortals to taste the nectar
of the gods, so found himself eternally hindered
from achieving his goals. An overhead projector
will often raise the specter
of our falling short. A scene that looks fine on paper
may be unrealizable by any director.
It's going to take more than a milligram of Catapres
to cure the Empress of this latest case of the vapors
brought on by the thought of being canceled;
her virtue-signaling capers
reminiscent of a she-goat in a spancel
who's convinced herself she's free of her fetters
even as she follows the goatherd to the letter.

If the truffle has never been known to tremble
before those hunting it down, it's because it's settled
for the opportunity to dissemble
afforded Molière's Tartuffe. The word "petal"
is essentially a term for a plate of metal
found in the artichoke, the artichoke given to extoll the virtues
of life confined to the shtetl
or the ghetto. At a Christmas party we might cajole
a girl to kiss under the mistletoe-bole
that once overhung
the soda dispenser. A few brave souls
will take on their being forced to bite their tongue
while the rest of us sidle
around the issue of the brank (a.k.a. scold's bridle).

11

Mark Antony's wife, Fulvia, would puncture
Tully's tongue with her hairpin so as to drive home
her point about trash talk. At a critical juncture
the artichoke would be reflected in the dome
of the Pantheon though the Hippodrome
in Tyre was deserted but for a single bucking bronc.
This was the era when serfs would comb
the forest for conk
alongside purple-striped Roman nerds and wonks
to whom they represented mere protozoa.
At the Honky Château a totally zonked
Bolan would sport a periwinkle feather boa.
That sea-snail dye also set off the hem
of the garment of the High Priest in Jerusalem.

12

The oak under which Abraham pitched his pavilion
wasn't chosen because it was a source
of divine power any more than the city of Ilion
was built around a horse
yet Tully's "spirit of the place" does reinforce
the idea of the *numen*
giving a nod in the direction of both Celtic and Norse
worldviews and serves to illumine
our human fascination with the superhuman.
Even as we acknowledge Hel to be the ruler
of the Norse version of "hell," we know albumin
lords it over us all. Our idle chat round a watercooler
may still spark a controversy
as to why men were turned into pigs by Circe.

13

The shaman who first saw the possibility of tinder
in a horse hoof fungus or punky log
is quite unlikely to have been a rescinder
of any law against castrating a hog.
Surely it would be a hard slog
for a rock band named after a dinosaur,
particularly if theatrical smoke and fog
has already consigned it to the days of yore.
The artichoke is, in the end, a folding door
that opens onto a vista
in which the Emperor (saddened, saddle-sore),
witnessed it being launched from a crude ballista
improvised by the Persians and sending a shock
wave through the defenders of Antioch.

14

What with that shitty crupper holding his saddle
in place the Emperor realizes it's *Polyporus
squamosus* he now straddles,
the great oak grove that lies before us
giving us druids *and* dryads. When Tyrannosaurus
Rex fell by the wayside, Bolan would molt
one periwinkle feather while a Greek chorus
waited in the wings to give him a jolt
of reality. There were roughly a hundred million volts
in play when Zeus struck the fire-monster, Typhon,
with a fiery thunderbolt,
a thunderbolt now functioning mostly as the hyphen
introduced as a matter of course
into an adjectival phrase such as "storm-force."

A student of the Father of Logic (a.k.a. Aristotle),
Theophrastus had nonetheless lost the knack
of reconciling a Gloucestershire Old Spot's mottle
with the broad strokes of a Wessex Saddleback.
The truffle, be it white or black,
looks as if it was casually dropped by a pig gelder
from the bloody grain sack
in which he once brought home his modest melder.
However fine a craftsman (part riveter, part welder),
behind an armadillo's scute,
most remarkable of all, according to Pliny the Elder,
is that a truffle seems to grow without a root.
From the tallest tree a thrush will try to take stock
of the situation. A mistle thrush (a.k.a. stormcock).

16

Now Pliny's depiction of druids in their white mantles
cutting down mistletoe with golden sickles
has the Emperor lean back on the cantle
of his saddle. The pig gelder with his mickle
of grain that's become a loaf of pumpernickel.
The divination of an hors d'oeuvre
in the midst of the artichoke's prickles
had to have taken a certain amount of nerve
and represented another steep learning curve.
I have been faithful to thee, Cynara! in my fashion
though it's true I've been known to swerve
towards rugelach and hamantaschen.
The only reason a thrush would ever swivel
on its sentry post is to be heard above the drivel.

For a stormcock will raise its voice above the racket
merely to exult
in its few words of Tungusic or Yakut.
The shaman at the center of a mushroom cult
may amass a following that will catapult
him into superstardom. Although he
did serve nectar to mortals, Tantalus added insult
to injury by offering his pasty-faced (a.k.a. doughy)
son to the gods. It's hard to be unshowy
while remaining defiant,
as an artichoke attests. With regard to David Bowie's
description of Bolan as "the greatest little giant,"
that sounds troublingly like a small child
patronizing another small child.

18

Deepwater oysters are small, we heard from Pliny,
because they're down in the dumps.
Marc Bolan died when his Mini
bounced off a railing and into a sycamore stump
on the South Circular. Hump, thump. Hump, thump.
The milky sap of spurge
all over a dead rump.
We know the male pig's sexual urge
is of a piece with our own to merge
the transient and the eternal;
Bolan was eternally on the verge
of cracking open the world and finding the kernel.
I think of Jupiter rattling his shield-rim
and the mistletoe forever going out on a limb.

19

Let's not forget that Frigg and Odin (a.k.a. Wodan)
were the parents of Thor, that other God of Thunder,
who first flashed when Lord Snowdon
photographed Bowie in 1978. No wonder,
so, when Cynara committed the social blunder
of sneaking home to see her folks,
Zeus threw her out with a force that would sunder
a mistletoe-festooned oak;
he flung Cynara down like a lightning stroke
and from the spot where she'd been hurled
the very first artichoke
had sprung up like a "Dandy in the Underworld,"
a symbol of earthly love to any squinter
through the mists of the solstice (a.k.a. midwinter).

Theophrastus may not have heard Mott the Hoople
kicking up a racket
in the flesh but Aristotle's star pupil
knew *Polyporus squamosus* was in a bracket
of its own. A version of *turdus ipse sibi malum cacat*
had been voiced by a medicine man
in Tungusic or Yakut
long before Erasmus; that a mistle thrush often ran
afoul of itself when it hit the can
may well underpin its ongoing squabble
with the pig that's been part of the oak-grove's plan
for world domination since a she-goat first hobbled
down to the watercooler through the thicket
beloved of the mistletoe-bearing buck (a.k.a. pricket).

No wonder "oak-sperm" is used of the viscous fluid
from the mistletoe-belt about the abdomen
of the oak tree druid after druid
has already scanned for an omen.
Theatrical smoke and fog have done yeoman
service in at least trying to muffle
the screams of the victims of Roman
legionaries practicing their ol' soft-shoe shuffle.
In Italy, the use of pigs to hunt for truffles
has been prohibited since 1985
on account of the damage caused when they snuffle
through a forest. Such is the self-generative drive
of that very truffle its scent mimics a hormone
in a male pig's saliva. The male pig's sex hormone.

Pablo Neruda: "Ode to the Artichoke"

A mild-mannered soul
in the guise of a militiaman,
the artichoke
stands tall, having thrown up
its own little turret,
keeping itself
intact
under
its scale armor.
On either flank
rogue vegetables
are beginning to waver,
becoming
earring-tendrils, cattails,
bulbs shifting position
in the subsoil,
the sleeping carrot
with its ginger mustache,
the vine
with its dried-out shoots
through which wine once flowed,
the cabbage
giving itself over
to trying on its mother's skirts,
the oregano
to scenting the whole world,

but the good old
artichoke's
still there in the garden,
still got up as a guerrilla fighter,
gleaming
like a hand grenade,
bursting with pride,
till one day
it's conscripted with the rest of its kind,
piled into a great wicker
hamper
and marched through the market
till its dream's realized—
it's in the army now!
Lined up for drill,
the artichokes have never seemed
so regimented
as at the fair,
men now
moving among the vegetable stalls
in their blanched shirts,
marshaling
the artichokes
row upon row,
shouting out order after order,
then the rifle-report
of a crate hitting the ground.
After which
Maria

comes along
with her basket,
herself cool as a cucumber,
picking out
the artichoke of artichokes,
giving it the once-over, holding it
up to the light as if it were an egg,
paying for it,
stuffing it
into her handbag
alongside a pair of shoes,
a head of cabbage,
and a bottle
of vinegar,
till
she enters her kitchen
and plunges it into a saucepan.
So the career
of this vegetable
known as the "artichoke,"
a vegetable
armed to the teeth,
ends
in relative peace
after which,
plate by armor-plate,
we strip away
its delectability
and are finally able to bite down hard

on the unseasoned
essence
of its tender heart.

Sure Thing

1

A rider doomed to flail in a blood-filled pit
may no longer rely on a martingale
to check his horse. I see through my own eye-slit
a rider doomed to flail
now so many attackers have managed to scale
the outer wall. Despite the close-knit
plates of our mail
we'll sooner or later submit
to a roundel-point. The Sultan will assail
us with such force a crossbow-bolt will unfailingly hit
the rider already doomed to flail.

2

In the midst of such an onslaught to hear the crank
of a single crossbow left you no less taut
than when we sat on a riverbank
in the midst of such an onslaught.
"Havoc," you said, "is wreaked rather than wrought."
I quite understand why you shrank
from the idea this was the first time we'd fought
just as I understood your "thanks but no thanks"
to my offer of homemade wild-caught
tuna sushi paired with a glass of sauvignon blanc
in the midst of such an onslaught.

3

Wearing a helmet-spike won't ward off the shit
showering a rider floundering in the blood-filled dike
between the city walls. Every nitwit
wearing a helmet-spike
is a look-alike
for the Emperor, a dead spit
giving him a new lease on life. An armorer will strike
when the iron's hot but his expansionism won't sit
well with Charlemagne and the First Reich.
Those flames that no faggot feeds, nor steel has lit,
are wearing a helmet-spike.

4

In the midst of such an onslaught from the Franks
or the Ottomans taking potshot
after potshot it's easy to see why your spirits sank
in the midst of such an onslaught
and why you've thought
it inappropriate to expose your flank
to Field Commander Mein Gott
never mind someone of a lesser rank.
It's also deemed bad luck to utter the word "apricot"
anywhere near a U.S. Marine Corps tank
in the midst of such an onslaught.

5

A nail from the true cross repurposed as a snaffle bit
by Constantine the Great leaves us at a loss
as to why anyone would counterfeit
a nail from the true cross
merely to serve as a gloss
on Zechariah and fulfill a prophecy in Holy Writ.
The bridle-makers of Byzantium continue to emboss
a cheekpiece with a motto that will indeed befit
a rider doomed to flail in a bloody fosse
wearing a helmet-spike that is—on the face of it—
another nail from the true cross.

A Quickie

In a hardtack factory
on Water Street
we entertain the suspicion that victory
is rarely if ever sweet

and we'll almost certainly founder
despite our long slog
through misadventure upon misadventure
too small to log,

suffering a far lesser want
than our County Tyrone neighbor, John King,
whom the Yandruwandha
took under their wing

after the demise
of Burke and Wills,
their pitching out along that far-flung Thames
in the hope they might somehow still

their compass in a gimbal
designed by Philo of Byzantium,
bemoaning how their twenty-six camels
were unresponsive to the rum

meant to revive their spirits,
John King troubled mostly by the grotesque
image of one camel spread
naked across a writing desk

with its eye sewn in needlepoint,
John King who would learn
how the Yandruwandha pound
the roasted spores of the Nardoo fern

with a mortar and pestle
into stuff almost as stiff
as his great-aunt's bustle
that might offer some brief respite even if

in a hardtack factory
on Water Street
we're confirmed in our suspicion that victory
is rarely if ever sweet.

Rosalind

Back when I was a man pretending to be a woman
pretending to be a man
I found myself able to summon

a range of emotions that ran
the gamut from common to not-so-common.
The checkout person at H Mart trying to scan

my fish sauce puts me in mind of a Roman
housewife trying to coax an eel into a copper pan.
The lamb with cumin

hails from Afghanistan.
"*Nomen est omen*," said Plautus. "*Nomen est omen*."
Plautus itself means "plodder" or "Kick the Can

Down the Road." Such was the acumen
of the 9th Legion they devised a plan
to introduce a diet of offal boiled in a sheep's rumen

to the already sluggardly Picts. In 82 A.D. the life span
of a sheep was almost as long as that of a human.
Things were rarely simpler, though, than

back when I was a man pretending to be a woman
pretending to be a man
who now found himself pretending to be a woman.

By the Time You Read This

By the time you read this I'll be gone
for a newspaper and quart of milk
never to return, a half-mowed lawn
leading to me as a scroll of silk

once led to the mulberry silkworm.
By the time you read this I'll be gone
AWOL in spite of the fact, in terms
of domesticity, I've outshone

even the heedful trumpeter swan
that spends five weeks constructing a nest.
By the time you read this I'll be gone
less because of some profound unrest

than my fascination with the Cree
and the sandhills of Saskatchewan
into which windswept immensity,
by the time you read this, I'll be long gone.

The Glow-Worm to the Mower

Since you're unlikely to astound
yourself by having more to save
than hay, small wonder you've not found
why wave upon successive wave

would summon, far inland, sea-sounds
from a dull scythe or sickle.
When Juliana and you downed
tools to lunch on cheese and pickles

atop the triangular mound
with its outcrop of hairy vetch
for which your meadow is renowned
it must have felt like the home stretch

to a safe harbor. Black horehound
in the sheugh. The sun a sea-gong.
All afternoon you would expound
on how a mower must be strong

while Juliana, tightly wound
as ever, slowly went off-script,
the vetch-garland with which she's crowned
having by dusk completely slipped,

the ties by which lovers are bound
also substantially weakened.
We mourn all those poor souls who've drowned
because our own inconstant beacons

have led to their running aground;
bear in mind it's by, and from, you
(and not the other way around)
we glow-worms steer and take our cue.

At the Grave of Chang and Eng

Though Snappy Lunch is closed all week
and we're quite bereft of a pork chop sandwich berth
Chang and Eng are still dancing cheek to cheek

in a grave near Mt. Airy that even now bespeaks
their own combined girth.
Though Snappy Lunch is closed all week

we revel in a rose-breasted grosbeak's
territory-staking song. Conjoined in death as in birth,
Chang and Eng are still dancing cheek to cheek

in a heaven filled with other kooks and geeks
who simply wouldn't cut it on earth.
Though Snappy Lunch is closed all week

that we're shut out lends it a greater mystique
and induces even a sense of mirth;
Chang and Eng are still dancing cheek to cheek

but to Nile Rodgers and Chic's "Le Freak."
So we revel most in knowing, for what it's worth,
though Snappy Lunch is closed all week
Chang and Eng are still dancing cheek to cheek.

Opossum

Though there's most likely a bailiff
on his way from Fancy Gap
to repossess
its off-road Jeep, this poser

opossum is ready to bluff
its way past any handicap.
Since its gray morning dress
befits a Royal Enclosure

it lifts itself rung by rung,
kicking it up a notch
till it's firmly ensconced at Ascot,

one of its young
ticking like a watch
from a pocket of its waistcoat.

Welcome to the Irish Alps

In memory of Charles Simic

That the Gallic tribes were the "people of the hills"
(sharing an Indo-European root with *collis*),
is an idea wherein their heirs in the Eastern Catskills
still find a smidgin of solace.

That the Gauls were the "people of the milky skin"
from a galaxy far, far away
that supplied Greece with boatloads of tin
is another concept that holds sway.

That the Gallic tribes were the "people of the woods"
(sharing an Indo-European root with *coill*),
is a theory on which the bronzers of pinecones

find themselves at odds with those who've stood
behind the notion, based on the Old Irish *gall*,
that the Gauls were the "people of the raised stone."

Three Deer, Sharon Springs, November 2020

Got up though they may be in heavy-duty gabardine
they cavort like fawn-devotees of Dionysus.
Their patron saint is Joseph of Cupertino,

the go-to guy for dunces
who'll make a run for it across a four-lane highway.
You have to admit they're tenacious,

holding out no less than goats or hee-haws
for a tidbit that's survived blight or powdery mildew.
The jury's hung as to whether the Woes

of the Pharisees amount to eight (as in Matthew)
or six (as in Luke).
A corner of the meadow

where a sky once lived is shown by that blue plaque;
the sky this morning's streaked with Coppertone
now the snow's been washing its dirty linen in public.

Nativity, 2020

Even a barn makes room for the fresh crop.
Even the cattle have drawn down their stores.
The mangold holds out nothing for even the grub.
Even the piebald sheep are waifs and strays.

Even the cart has been kicked to the curb.
Even the harness is under some stress.
Sweat has cured even the haft of a three-tined graip.
Even the three Wise Men will grimly steer

even if falling foul of mission-creep.
In the grain-bin not even the mouse stirs
though even a mouse may be a greedy wee gorb.
Even the ass shimmies to Richard Strauss

even as the hay shimmies from the crib.
Even a prophet sometimes misconstrues
the trickle-down effect found in even a groop.
Even a camel may be moved to tears.

Even the three Wise Men are shooting craps.
Even the horse has its head in the stars.
The mountain, even the mountain, is up for grabs.
Even the river is grasping at straws.

The Wheel Invents the Road

The wheel invents the road.
You made me what I am.
We met as the Granta rather improbably flowed
into the crook of the Cam

and the fish cast their own net.
Like you . . . like you, hoping for the best.
That must be why all bets
were off when your own hope chest

was found to contain a goose lamp, a swatch
of Belgian linen, a skirt with a frayed hem,
a pocket watch
with a wonky winding stem

that may or may not have belonged to Burt,
a brandy flask, a spider plant,
and a billet-doux from a little squirt
who'd tried to get in your pants.

Did the fig invent the wasp or the wasp the fig?
The hornbill invented the casque.
Barely had we taken a swig
from the flask

than McCartney had dropped *Flowers in the Dirt*
and we stood in the light of the goose lamp
to tally one kid's growth spurt
on a doorjamb,

then found ourselves taken to task
for having brought the other to see *Hedwig*.
Trask . . . Stephen Trask.
The hermaphrodite brig

invented the skull and crossbones T-shirt.
Did the ant invent the acacia or the acacia the ant?
A buffalo has been known to animadvert
on Immanuel Kant

and his version of *adaequatio intellectus ad rem*,
an oxpecker to drink Scotch
while listening to Rani Arbo and Daisy Mayhem
kicking it up a notch.

The diaphragm does indeed invent the chest.
The loudspeaker fleshes out its cabinet.
The other day I heard you suggest
the Celtic tree alphabet

you pronounce as Og-*ham*
is a kind of Universal Product Code.
You made me what I am.
The wheel invents the road.

The Riders

Some sigh for those nine bean rows
Some the heavenly abode
Some sigh for the binary
Some the binary code
Some load a hermaphrodite brig
With a cargo of tin
Some ride with Quanah Parker
Some ride against the wind
And those of us who've ridden the white horse
In our own expeditionary force
Now weep that history must run its course
Now weep that history must run its course

Some sigh for the Café d'Alsace
Some for telling it slant
Some sigh for brave Ulysses
Some Ulysses S. Grant
Some can't believe that you're for real
I think I've got you sussed
Some ride upon the railroad
For some it rides on us
And those of us who've ridden the white horse
In our own expeditionary force
Now weep that history must run its course
Now weep that history must run its course

Some still sigh for Art Blakey
Some sigh for how he rolled
Some sigh for Acapulco
Some Acapulco Gold
Some hold a piercing on their tongue
Some a burning coal
Some ride in on a donkey
Some ride out on a pole
And those of us who've ridden the white horse
In our own expeditionary force
Now weep that history must run its course
Now weep that history must run its course

Coywolves

The sight of one crossing my yard—all copper-zinc—
in broad daylight, is etched on my eye.
It's mostly at night, though, when they snag

a hapless deer, their voices are raised on high.
No sooner do they corner a woodchuck or raccoon
than their cover of "Ghost Riders in the Sky"

resounds from here to Oregon.
The version I myself favor, to kick off a road trip,
is Frankie Laine's of 1963. Others reckon

Johnny Cash to be preeminent. Still others heap
praise on Elvis Presley and Burl Ives.
This midnight mix of yodels and yippie-yi-oohs

may derive
not from a whole pack but a single pair.
In Alaska a hunter's been known to set out knives

covered in ice-blood on which coywolves will pare
themselves down to the bone.
Though this may be no more than a brouhaha

over competing claims to a garbage bin
that'll set off the neighbor's motion
detector camera, we hear it as both a paean

of praise from a Mission
featuring a mosaic
of Saint Francis and the wolf and a muezzin's

call to prayer from an unlikely mosque.
Frankie Laine did invite me once to cowrite a song
but I stupidly declined because I can't read music.

A Graveyard in New England

Although we've spent so much time clearing fields
it seems a plow does little more than scratch
the surface of the land we'd hoped would yield
one hundred pumpkins from the pumpkin patch

and represent a hundredfold increase.
Although we've spent so much time clearing fields
and taken out quite a lengthy lease
on this hacked rim of the Canadian Shield

only recently has it been revealed
it's not just in our beds lovers must bundle.
Although we've spent so much time clearing fields
it seems we've simultaneously trundled

granite blocks, boulders, and boundary terms
into a single tract in which we've sealed
their fates and are quite bent on holding firm
although we've spent so much time clearing fields.

The Rain

Just moments after you offered your hand to the rain
the rain would seem to palm you off
with the overflowing train
of a wedding gown and the unbleached coif

worn by Joan of Arc
under a steel casque. The only ray
of hope was a hoof spark
on the road to Vouvray

after the hailstorm
of June 2013 when the grape crop
pretty much came a cropper. A swarm
of bees so loves a photo op

it will hang out its shingle on 62nd Street
while waiting for Otello
to warm up his thunder sheet.
You know Toscanini played second cello

for the toffee-nosed toffs
attending the premiere? The Met might refrain
from letting a horse tread the boards in *Godunov*
did it not take more than a rein

to halt such trends. If a touch of cadmium yellow
is enough to elicit snow or sleet
from a canvas surely some Robin Goodfellow
could have launched not only a horse but a fleet

of chariots by way of the scene shop.
That was back in 2010, when it was indeed the norm
for a statue to swap
itself out for Il Commendatore, a cloud to transform

itself into a woman way
reminiscent of Julie Harris in *The Lark*,
the woman now dismounting her dapple-gray
in the dawn-dark,

consoling it with a snort of grain
and leading it to an overflowing trough
just moments after you offered your hand to the rain
and she seemed to palm you off.

What Snow Is For

For reminding us of what might disappear
night after night without leaving any trace—
the buck dropping a single handkerchief-ear
to signal the start of a chariot race

that may only ever end in Antioch
and a loud prig's besting by a local prince.
For the stadium's collective *ach* or *och*
as the cycle turns implacably to rinse

across the blur of the cemetery grounds
where a head's still often dashed against a stone.
For rounding out the coywolf doing his rounds
with that much-vaunted consistency of tone

yet underlining what lies beyond our reach
is a function of the margin, not the page.
For having us cry out in joy, each to each,
without the least compunction to act our age.

For telling just how far it is to the shed.
For telling how cavalierly we say "white."
For daring us to be in over our heads.
For a laundry room wall nicked with the kids' heights.

For revealing religion is unrevealed
to the preacher letting off a little steam.
For completely leveling the playing field
on which we'll happily take one for the team.

For second-guessing the slalom through the glens
on which that buck will lead us a merry chase.
For the old Panavision wide-angle lens
that shows him to be quite the chariot-ace.

For falling from a tree with a muted thump
onto a sheet already spread out for fruit.
For convincing us we're now over the hump.
For allowing a threatened plant to take root.

For putting the skids on our putting the skids
on the idea we're brothers under the skin.
For drawing up that blank contract with our kids
with the sole stipulation all count as kin.

For taking the part of the partial eclipse.
For insisting that no flaw's a fatal flaw.
For having its own name on everyone's lips.
For establishing as equal before the law

a buck whose motivations we misconstrue
and a threatened sprig on which he loves to browse.
For proving every line's somewhat out of true
in the chamber from which we may one day rouse.

Let the Hare Sit

Indivisible from the form
of Méret Oppenheim's fur-lined cup and saucer;
at the highest point of a hill farm
she's about to lay into Geoffrey Chaucer
when something puts the heart across her—
the baying of a hound
where a road has run itself into the ground.

Not even that hound's jubilant woo-hoo
can have us soar above the sodden;
a neuron is condemned to the neural pathway.
When a hare loped out of James IV's tent at Flodden
it would stand in for the downtrodden
of centuries to come
and the tide of billhooks against which we've swum.

From time to time a captive may indeed be forced
to throw off her fetters;
having made their marks on the hoarfrost
of the meadow, the spaniels and setters
and other go-getters
must now decide if they should turn back
or resign themselves to trying to stay on track.

The music accompanying the death pangs
of a hare is always composed by Bernard Herrmann;
lying in as she is under the hedge bank
she is supremely well positioned to determine
something about the Old High German
word for the "stoat"
now turning up the collar of her winter coat.

From time to time a captive may rise above the fray
as teal blue complements burnt umber;
the hare will often get off scot-free
precisely because she'll appear to lumber
while the hounds that think they have her number
are following at such a clip
she'll almost inevitably give them the slip.

It used to be that anyone in it for the long haul
would win out over a sprinter;
nowadays she peers through a door-hole
where the sun at midwinter
makes every last one of us a squinter
across the landscape told at a slant
where many would benefit from a corneal transplant.

Let the hare sit while the bouncers, Spot and Scout,
are checking if she's a paid-up member;
her erect scut
has many a time glowed like an ember
in the dead center of December
even as the sun has been known to rub
shoulders with the earth in a basement club.

How painstakingly Albrecht Dürer would hatch
and crosshatch to perfectly render her fur pattern;
just because she'll scratch an itch
doesn't make her a slattern.
The moon may be in conjunction with Saturn
yet Venus, Jupiter, and Mars wait
patiently in line for a chance to mate.

In Dürer's *The Holy Family with Three Hares*
the hares are doomed to forever scoot and scutter;
if they represent Mary's leaning less towards Eros
than Eostre they also speak to her utter
contempt for the idea of a shutter
that will block
her view of the fertile Lowlands and the distant loch.

Chaucer's portrayal of the Wife of Bath
is of a piece with Les Blank's *Gap-Toothed Women*;
it takes more than slicing through its pith
to get to the core of a persimmon.
As for the sun, imagine including him in
the meet and greet of a megalithic tomb
only to find him systematically working the room.

Hardly if ever, in the Annals, would a captive dare
fall in love with her captor;
when they brought Dame Hare to the White Tower
and clapped her
in irons they thought they were closing a chapter
rather than flinging open the blinds
on anything and everything that may spring to mind.

Whilst the Ox and Ass

Whilst the ox and ass are granted the gift of speech,
having knelt in adoration of a child,
it would represent a breach
of decorum were we to listen in. For all those exiled

from their native lands, all those gagged
whilst the ox and ass are granted the gift of speech,
all those who've dragged
their belongings over a border, it's still a reach

to take in why two lambs might cry out each to each
across the crevasse of a manger.
Whilst the ox and ass are granted the gift of speech
they almost immediately sense danger

and, like us, are almost immediately struck dumb.
"Beseech" is the word. The lamb will beseech
and beseech us never to keep mum
whilst the ox and ass are granted the gift of speech.

from Irish Slavers

for Shane McCrae

3

Time and time again the Irish Coast Guard
has rescued a Phelim who's run aground on Gola . . .
In 1939 there was a U-boat sequestered

in virtually every cove between Killybegs and Killala:
nowadays I make do with a teenager
in a New York café sending back her Coca-Cola

lest it put her in danger.
"Dirtier by far than clarts," she's saying, "is glaur."
A scarlet tanager

blown across the Atlantic and spotted on Cape Clear
puts me in mind of a slave castle
in Ghana administered by Richard Brew from Clare.

5

On the day before the storming of the Bastille
the captain of the *Experiment* opens his Gazetteer
to plot a course away from the bustle

of the Thames. The rib-tickling Costard
in *Love's Labour's Lost* proves to be a polymath
but the Creighton Hale who costarred

in *The Cat and the Canary* will see a falling-off
in his reputation, playing bit parts
that are largely uncredited. Froth . . . Moth . . .

It's not only pirates
who're likely to peg
us as cogs in the wheel. Abrade. Abrade. Abrade.

Though we may still be at the beck
and call of those Company of Merchants imbeciles,
at least we'll die with harness on our back.

6

The chance of living on an installment plan
is one for which we're all so eager
we'll happily dive into a divan

without a thought for *le vinaigre*.
That woman throwing a kidney into the pan?
Her husband's to Aleppo gone, master of the Tiger,

to beat some sense into the Syrians.
Can you hear him calling from far across the waves?
What bloody man is that? What bloody man?

7

Another piece in the puzzle
is William Ronan, the Cape Coast bigwig,
running a quizzical

eye over the latest intake of "wenches" and "bucks"
as if they were no more than swine
cast before pearls. Slopped, indeed, like pigs

in their belowdecks swoon
many will be lost in transit as, on his pillowed bench,
the coxswain

contemplates a glass of *bolleponge*
flavored with nutmeg and lemon zest.
At Annamaboe Castle, Brew's piper plays "Banish

Misfortune" while we get half-soused.
Ms. Glaur and Phelim are drawn into the pantomime
in which we've seized

on the idea it might blow over if we all keep mum
about Brew and the bestial
Ronan presiding over murder and mayhem.

9

Time and time again we've emerged unscathed
from the wreckage of an *Experiment*.
The bowsprit. The barrel-staves.

The swivel from a swivel-mount.
The waiter may seem to be no more than a knave
who'll replace that Coke in a New York minute

but the way he cuts a broad swath
through the café also puts me in mind
of a song—the song still in us as we go to the grave.

13

One of the pastry chefs will use a mortar and pestle
to grind cinnamon and cardamom.
The whip? It's made from a pizzle.

A pizzle, ma'am,
is the cured penis of a bull.
Quite unlikely to kill you outright. Merely maim.

It would be a pity to let anything cast a pall
over our living on the Never-Never
with our friends Dick and Bill

and those spear carriers from the court of Navarre.
Go on. Spell it out. A-L-K-A-L-O-I-D.
Good against yellow fever

and the unlikely event there'll be a glut
in the market. Dick and Bill and their ilk will guzzle
a ball of punch as soon as a Kool-Aid.

15

Like Macbeth, we all wear business casual.
Could the 1927 version of *The Cat and the Canary*
have it over the 1939 remake? When a passel

of hogs go on the rampage in Perth and Kinross
they'll uproot Birnam Wood. The aftermath
of chronic gonorrhea

is a dishonorable discharge from the mickey or muff
that's known specifically as "gleet."
We still subscribe to the myth

we might as readily dispel our guilt
as add quinine to our rhubarb gin custard.
Time and time again the sky has left under a cloud.

Winslow Homer: *The Veteran in a New Field*

Quite apart from the Union Army jacket and canteen
that dominate the foreground,
the very cross of the galluses
on his back might mark him as a target

for the many still keen
to remember their kin downed
at Appomattox. Some blisters never grow calluses
just as some townsfolk never grasp the argot

of a scythe's "tang" and "snaith."
The veteran lays into the head-high barley
as if he might indeed stand firm

against these serried ranks of wraiths
with whom there's no hope of sitting down to parley
never mind coming to terms.

A Least Bittern

For as long as we could recall, what would prevail
was the wind against which we might but vent
as it tossed us to and fro . . .
Because the Irish had been in a holding pattern

for as long as we could recall, we loved a powerful
storm that, in Galway or Clare, had us find
a common nighthawk, a red-eyed vireo,
or a least bittern

blown clear across the Atlantic
on a wing and a prayer . . .
This was not to speak of our blue-eyed ancestors

venturing out from the Pontic
Steppe and borne along mostly by their own uproar.
Their cry a rusty hinge. Their yellow sou'westers.

2

As for our native bellower, he was inclined to skirt
each and every issue like a plank road
skirting the wetlands; much as he roared like a bull
and beat his own drum

our native bellower could also point his bill skywards
and do a fair impression of a reed
indeed pointing its bill
towards the sky. From the flooded scriptorium

of a ruined monastery he came to favor
plangency over plainsong. A monk intent on a scrap
of vellum had always afforded him a hefty

dose of reality, given that a feather
from his left wing best suited the right-handed scribe whereas
a feather from his right suited the lefty.

3

For the moment we must make do with a pinch hitter
rather than an acknowledged ace
yet this least bittern may encourage us to burst
out of the vale of tears with which,

for the moment, we must make do, having us shatter
our illusions like the sheet of ice
by which Satan's still held midbreast,
exchanging our low wattage

pietism for an honest-to-god
barn burner, trading in our moans and groans
and the sense everything's dependably lackluster

for the chance we'll not only survive another decade
but stage a comeback, like the kickline crane
or the falcon with his brass knuckle-duster.

Hardtack

That a ship's biscuit might yet see us through
our circumnavigation of the globe
is testimony to its shelf life, true,
though your nonchalant doffing a bathrobe

makes me think you're also playing for keeps.
That a ship's biscuit might yet see us through
may be traced back partly to Samuel Pepys
and his time in the navy, partly to

our weevil-sense it's easier to chew
when first softened behind the lower lip.
That a ship's biscuit might yet see us through
from the time we weighed anchor at Pike Slip

to our pretty much having learned the ropes
vindicates our taking the longer view
and persisting, pretty much, in the hope
that a ship's biscuit might yet see us through.

The MRI

Again and again we'll put our shoulder
to the wheel
on which we're broken. Stretched out at the heart
of a replica of the stone
sarcophagus we once believed to "eat flesh,"
we still have a straight

shot at the Strait
of Gibraltar. Where we first found a shoulder
to cry on. Long before the flash
of an iron-rimmed wheel
on a limestone
pavement. Where we first had a little heart

to heart.
Where we first developed our sense of the straight
and narrow. Threw the first stone.
First rubbed shoulders
with pigment traders. First made a color wheel.
First thought to flush

dyes through our own flesh
so as to map what lies within our hearts.
First reinvented the wheel
that will run straight
only with a camber. First gave the cold shoulder
to a pigment trader. First chipped away at limestone

till it actually looked like stone.
First assigned a shoulder flash
to the Airborne Division. First deigned to shoulder
the blame for what happened in the heart
of Galicia. Long before we learned to lie straight
as a die though the planets wheel

and wheel
about us. Before we first secured a lodestone
to a merchantman. First entered the home straight
where ore is crushed in the flosh
as the heart
is oft-times crushed. First put our shoulder

to that great wheel. Saw Anu in the flesh.
First learned that a stone-faced doctor has the heart
to give it to us straight from the shoulder.

Joy in Service on Rue Tagore

1

As I enter a doctor's office
on 57th between Eighth and Ninth
a rat comes zigzag towards me like a powder-fuse
towards a keg. Every three months

I'd meet Emile in Le Petit Prince
or another high-end restaurant in Algiers.
In Le Normand we bought foie gras by the ounce
even as we rearranged the deck chairs;

it seemed rats given a high dosage of the amaranth
dye found in maraschino cherries
would develop tumors

so he favored mint to garnish his crème de menthe.
Bottoms up, old boy. Cheers.
If he didn't have fresh mint he'd extemporize.

2

If he didn't have fresh mint he'd extemporize
with something from the diplomatic pouch
to simultaneously pep up and put dampers
on our spirits. One woman flashed the badge

of a nipple but looked askance
when I took it in. Once it was all cloak and dagger.
We were all undercover once,
until Emile's headstrong *cri de coeur*

against my using the hand he kept in the fridge
of his apartment on Rue Tagore
to plant a fingerprint on a doorknob chez Ducasse.

In those years it was so much easier to fudge
the evidence, before DNA and my own dodgy ticker,
the years spent chained to a briefcase.

3

The years I spent with a briefcase
chained to my wrist
are as nothing now, those most pervicacious
young creatures I encouraged to do their worst

having long since renounced
their claims or fallen foul of Special Ops.
Every October Emile would make syrup of quince.
He and I have both been toodle-pipped

at the post
by the mediocracy, the closest I now come to a stab
of joy itself being somewhat amorphous—

the fleeting smile, the blood test
proving negative that lends a bounce to my step
as I leave a doctor's office.

The Mourner

From deep within my grave
I must have been hoping to present less of a target
to those who would make me an object of grief.
The use of ergot

to loosen the birth knot
and generally bring on labor
had also proved invaluable to hastening my end.
That silent "b" in Lefebvre

bruited the space in which an archer might train
his ash arrow on an ash tree.
I was able to gauge this most recent arc

from the green stain
where a mourner had now gone down on one knee
the better to find his mark.

The Castle of Perseverance

1

As one's eyes became accustomed to the glimmer
of light from the single candle
the interior of the chamber
gradually loomed, and little by little we got a handle

on the strange medley of things
heaped one upon the other. A second candle
and an electric torch showed two effigies of a king,
ebony-black, gold sandaled,

bearing staff and mace; ornamental caskets;
finely carved chairs; a throne;
beneath our very eyes, on the threshold,

a wishing-cup in alabaster; baskets;
stools in all shapes, inlaid with precious stones;
overturned parts of chariots glinting with gold.

2

All this suggested the property-room of an opera
set in a world now long since vanished . . .
Was it a tomb or merely a cache the grave-robbers
had already banished

beyond the realm
of their own possibility? So much else has vanished
from our lives: the art of steam-bending elm
for a chariot wheel; the Spanish

sword repurposed by Hannibal Barca
against the Romans; the flint razor taking a scalp;
the appetite for killing without a qualm;

the proto-parka
worn by a Copper Age denizen of the Alps;
the parlor where my mother would be embalmed.

3

This was the room in which I first heard the rustle
of crepe as she began her journey
on the carousel,
its "little battle" summoning a tourney

for which we all must enter the lists.
The jury may be out as to whether our final journey
is circular or linear but that an ovarian cyst
would condemn my mother to a gurney

is beyond question. It's when a body has a quarrel
with itself it will most likely break a lance
just as it's wreath-makers who most likely perpetuate

the idea a bay tree must look to its laurels.
Never do carousel horses prance
more emphatically than at a phantom starting gate.

4

Though the armchairs were fitted with antimacassars
to ward off the oil Lord Byron would once bracket
"incomparable," the threat now came from geezers
in drainpipe trousers and drape jackets

who slicked their hair with Brylcreem and pig grease.
I was already exercised by the fact "bracket"
might derive from a term for a codpiece
while the very thought of a "placket"

was enticingly off-limits.
Amid the nested coffins covered in hieroglyphs
was *A Dictionary of Rhyming Slang*;

my father, in dungarees and striped simmit,
may have detected a faint whiff
of soapberry scented with lavender or ylang-ylang.

5

Some of the patterns on a zebra
are reminiscent of the shadows cast by Venetian
blinds or an Elizabethan doublet slashed by a sabre
yet they're zebra through and through. The secretion

of silk by a worm
had Marco Polo, himself an eminent Venetian,
go to considerable lengths to reaffirm
his faith in the process of accrual and accretion

that culminated in our good room's Formica
sideboard and the Parker Knoll
wingback chair with a slight overhang

in which a magpie (*Pica pica*)
had amassed its own trove of paper money, coal, gunpowder,
and gunpowder tea from the Tang.

6

Despite suffering from a gammy
chimney and soot, the boy king was still able to pivot
on his chariot. Too early to benefit from chemo,
my mother had little more than an ounce of civet

from the apothecary; as she flew over Mont Blanc
her plane began to pitch and pivot
as if she were riding a bronc.
Attached to the saddle by a strap with a brass rivet,

the stirrup would almost solely account for the feudal
system by which a lord
would grant a lady her heartfelt wish

for the whole courtly kit and caboodle
and it wouldn't seem in the least untoward
for that rivet to turn up in the stomach of a fish.

7

Particularly if the boy king had set out along a river
that had spread itself so thin over the gravel
there was barely room for a salmon to further
its sole ambition, that being to travel

back to precisely where it was spawned,
working its way back over that self-same gravel
to that self-same icy pond.
When my mother's friend began to mentally unravel

she would quote those lines by Edmund Blunden
about the hop-poles standing in cones
over the frozen lake;

it looked as if her own trip to London
would have to be postponed
since the stab of pain had given way to a bellyache.

8

Any self-respecting Westminster Abbey
would know the route from the Elephant and Castle
to Regent's Park where a male hippo
captured on the Nile has been seen to offer a tassel

of corn as a love token
to another hippo; that L'Enfant de Castile
has no connection left my mother heartbroken;
my father was no less her vassal

than a Wade donkey burdened by two panniers
of more or less equal heft.
The feeling I had ever so slightly tipped

the balance was all the uncannier
(and left me all the more bereft)
now I realized a boy king might rest easy in his crypt.

9

Particularly if the boy king knows a donkey connives
again and again with a Bactrian camel
to eat rope, sandals, and even canvas
that's not properly secured; to be untrammeled

by this medley of things heaped
one upon the other is to fly that Sopwith Camel
over the South Tyrol. Our denizen of this steep
mountain pass showed severe wear of the enamel

of his teeth and advanced periodontitis
caused by a diet heavy in einkorn wheat,
ibex, another big-eyed deer in blue Murano glass;

these were all part of the detritus
of Belleek, Waterford crystal, a Murano parakeet
the magpie had somehow amassed.

10

Despite suffering from Lyme disease, our denizen
of the Alps, Ötzi, had more pressing issues,
chief among them being how to relieve the tension
caused by an arrowhead lodged in the deep tissue

of his back; that was why he would crouch
like a woman about to bring forth issue
or Lord Vishnu posing on his Naugahyde couch
at the New Year festival of Vishu;

my mother herself reclined behind the lace curtain
of an avalanche
in this whatnot-strewn Alpine pass

where she decided to go for a Burton
and ditched the biplane; a dove with an olive branch,
a Murano peacock; an ashtray of Benares brass.

11

Some of the patterns in the sixty-one tattoos found on Ötzi
suggest they were markers
for acupuncture; the day he set off on his odyssey
around the Naugahyde couch and the Parker

Knoll was his last day; some still subscribe
to the theory he missed the marker
of a boundary between his and a neighboring tribe
and things took a turn that was altogether darker;

as for the boy king at the heart of the clutter,
a wheel of steam-bent elm may well have gained
on a wheel of steam-bent ash

for, though our candles had begun to gutter,
it was still clear such wounds as he had sustained
were consistent with his being in a chariot crash.

12

Though the armchairs were themselves a memorial
to the court of petty session
over which my mother so often presided, the mural
in the boy king's tomb seemed to freshen

under this unfamiliar light, the curvature of his spine
to briefly relent. Now that her own session
was timing out, my mother would cross the finish line
in what proved less her transgression

than the carousel's inherent tendency to teeter
on some brink. As my mother set her amuletic wand
on those three Staffordshire flying ducks

I noticed a hole in the back of her windcheater
that seemed to correspond
pretty much exactly to where the arrow had struck.

13

This was the room in which Griselda
would become emblematic of wifely perseverance
as surely as each carousel
horse made its return appearance

and its rider would once again tilt
at a brass ring. Even if we understood perseverance
has no intrinsic merit we admired a cottage built
to withstand a famine clearance

or eviction prompted by the sheer malice
of a landlord; descendants of his tenants still nursed
a grievance for Jack Adair; at a no-frills

version of a picture palace
like the Olympic Cinema, Moy, *The Pharaoh's Curse*
and *Land of the Pharaohs* shared a double bill.

14

All this suggested we might yet disentangle
the original beauty
of *Cottages near Dungloe, County Donegal*
by J. H. Craig from a reproduction my often snooty

mother had nonetheless given pride of place
in the good room. For we knew beauty
may indeed replicate itself just as a chariot race
may do double duty

as a plot device. Among Vishnu's avatars are a turtle
and a colossal boar
sporting an unmacassared bristle-comb

and, as it happens, a mother now given to hurtle
across the Axminstered floor
of the Hippodrome.

15

As one's eyes became accustomed to the glisten
of light we were nonetheless flummoxed
by the extent of the debris field from the collision
of a chariot with a sandy hummock

that denotes where several narratives converge.
As for the extent to which we're generally flummoxed
we need look no further than our urge
to examine the contents of every fish's stomach

for a clue to our own status.
Leaving the lotus-prowed boat with two magical oars
on which my mother might cross the foam

we would close the hole, lock the wooden lattice
which had been placed upon the door,
mount our donkeys, and start for the gates of Rome.

Acknowledgments

Acknowledgments are due to the editors of the following, in which versions of some of these poems first appeared: *14*, *Arena* (RTÉ), *Exit 13*, *Harper's*, *Heat*, *The Hopkins Review*, *The Irish Times*, *Liberties*, *London Review of Books*, *The New York Review of Books*, *The New Yorker*, *One Hand Clapping*, *Poetry Birmingham Literary Journal*, *Poetry London*, *Poetry Please* (BBC Radio 4), *The Poetry Review*, *Porlock*, *Raritan*, *The Telegraph*, *TLS*, *The Verb* (BBC Radio 3).

"The Belfast Pogrom: Some Observations" was written under commission by University College Dublin and Poetry Ireland for Poetry as Commemoration 2022. "When the Italians" was included in *Walter de la Mare: Critical Appraisals*, edited by Yui Kajita, Angela Leighton, and A. J. Nickerson, and published by Liverpool University Press in 2022. "The Glow-Worm to the Mower" was included in *Companions of His Thoughts More Green: Quatercentenary Poems for Andrew Marvell* edited by David Wheatley and published by Broken Sleep Books in 2022. "Nativity, 2020" and "Whilst the Ox and Ass" were printed as Christmas cards by Peter Fallon of the Gallery Press in 2020 and 2022 respectively. "A Least Bittern" was included in *Eamon at 80*, a festschrift for Eamon Grennan published by the Gallery Press in 2022. Several of these poems appeared, alongside watercolors by Philip Pearlstein, in *The Castle of Perseverance*, published by Enitharmon Editions in 2022. Several others were included in *Sure Thing*, published as a Lighthouse Poetry Pamphlet in 2022. Yet others appeared on *Highlights of the Low Life*, an album of poems and songs by Paul Muldoon and Rogue Oliphant, which came out in 2022 from Soul Selects records.